The Prank Sisters

Story by Fiona Hardy

Illustrations by Monique Dong

The Prank Sisters

Text: Fiona Hardy
Publishers: Tania Mazzeo and Eliza Webb
Series consultant: Amanda Sutera
  Hands on Heads Consulting
Editor: Annabel Smith
Designer: Jess Kelly
Project designer: Danielle Maccarone
Illustrations: Monique Dong
Production controller: Renee Tome

NovaStar

Text © 2024 Cengage Learning Australia Pty Limited
Illustrations © 2024 Cengage Learning Australia Pty Limited

ISBN 978 0 17 033422 8

Cengage Learning Australia
Level 5, 80 Dorcas Street
Southbank VIC 3006 Australia
Phone: 1300 790 853
Email: aust.nelsonprimary@cengage.com

For learning solutions, visit **cengage.com.au**

Printed in China by 1010 Printing International Ltd
1 2 3 4 5 6 7 28 27 26 25 24

Nelson acknowledges the Traditional Owners and Custodians of the lands of all First Nations Peoples. We pay respect to Elders past and present, and extend that respect to all First Nations Peoples today.

Contents

Chapter 1

A Long Morning Ahead

Abby and her twin sister Zoe dragged another chair across the lounge room. The legs of the chair made a loud squeal over the floorboards.

Mum appeared in the doorway. "It's too early on a Saturday for all this noise. What's going on?"

"We're moving the furniture around in the room," Abby explained, pushing her curly hair away from her face.

"We're pranking Dad," Zoe said. "We saw it on *Pranking Superstars*. Some kids reversed all the furniture in their dad's office and won Prank of the Week!"

Mum sighed. "Our life isn't an online video."

Abby went to the couch next and pushed. She shoved too hard, and the couch bumped a side table. The plant on the table started to wobble.

Mum ran over and caught the plant before it fell. "No more moving furniture," she said.

"But we're *bored*," Zoe said, flopping on the couch. "How long until Grandma comes over?"

"She won't be here until midday," Dad said, walking into the room. He stared at the furniture, looking confused.

Abby groaned.

Mum said, "You need to find something better to do this morning than messing up the lounge room. Or any other room in the house."

"You could make birthday cupcakes for Grandma," Dad said. "And your birthday present for her is still in the brown paper bag on the hallway table waiting for you to wrap it."

Abby and Zoe were proud. They had saved up and bought Grandma a beautiful vase from an antique shop. She would love it.

"You can do anything, as long as it's not a prank," Mum said.

Zoe and Abby slouched off to their rooms, past the brown paper bag in the hallway.

Chapter 2

The Pranks Begin

Zoe was in her bedroom, trying very hard not to think about pranking, but she was so bored. Her tablet was broken and getting repaired. She'd run out of art supplies. And she'd read all of her books, twice.

All she could think about was pranking. There was nothing left to do except come up with a way to prank Abby.

After each episode of *Pranking Superstars*, the hosts would ask viewers to send in their prank ideas. The hosts then created videos of their favourite ones.

The twins had sent in 32 ideas so far. They had a box of props in the study. They also had a secret kit each, full of things just to prank the other one.

Zoe's collection was in a box she had hidden behind her big winter jackets in the wardrobe. She looked through the box, and sneezed when a feather tickled her nose.

It gave her an idea.

Zoe was smiling about her plan when she opened her bedroom curtains.

There was a scary face at the window, staring at her! Zoe screamed and dropped to the floor. Her heart was beating fast. Then she heard Abby laughing.

Zoe got up slowly on her hands and knees to look at the face again.

It wasn't a real person after all. It was a picture of a screaming face, with big black eyes. It looked like something out of a movie.

Zoe couldn't believe her sister had pranked her first. But her plan to get Abby back was even better.

Abby was back in her room, giggling to herself. She was thrilled that she had done the first prank of the day, and it had gone exactly as planned.

Still, Abby thought Zoe had sounded pretty scared when she screamed, so she wanted to find her and make sure she was okay. But Zoe wasn't in her bedroom, or the kitchen, or the lounge room.

Mum was in the study. Abby asked her, "Have you seen Zoe?"

"No," Mum said. "And I heard a scream before. There had better not be any pranking happening. And don't forget to wrap Grandma's present!"

Abby was too busy looking for Zoe to reply. She decided to look outside and headed to the back door.

Abby didn't notice the length of string tied around the door handle.

The other end of the string was tied to a bucket sitting above the door. The bucket was full of feathers from the chicken coop.

Abby opened the door.

The door pulled at the string, and the bucket tipped over.

One second later, Abby was covered in a puff of stinky, fluffy chicken feathers.

Chapter 3

The Gravy Milk

Abby knew *exactly* where her sister
was now. Zoe was rolling around on the
grass in the backyard, laughing at her.
The chickens were looking at Zoe strangely.
Chickens don't really get pranks.

Abby spat a feather out of her mouth.
She was dirty, smelly and annoyed.

"Just you wait," Abby said, glaring at Zoe.
"*I'm* going to be the Pranking Superstar
today."

Half an hour later, Abby stepped out of the shower. She had spent all that time getting the feathers out of her curls and thinking of a good prank.

Abby knew Zoe always had a hot chocolate for morning tea on weekends. So, when nobody was around, Abby snuck into the kitchen.

First, she emptied out the chocolate powder from the tin. Next, she filled the tin with gravy powder.

Smiling, Abby got two tubs of yoghurt out of the fridge and yelled out loud enough for her sister to hear, "I'm hungry!"

"Me too!" Zoe said, as she came thumping down the hallway to the kitchen.

Abby held out a yoghurt for Zoe.

Zoe stared at her sister. "No way," she said, suspiciously. "I bet you've done something to it. I'll just have my usual hot chocolate."

Abby tried not to laugh. Zoe made her drink, then took a big gulp.

"Eww!" she sputtered. "What did you do to my hot chocolate?"

"Yes, Abby," Dad said, peering around the kitchen door and making them jump. "What DID you do to Zoe's hot chocolate?"

The girls went quiet.

"Did Abby prank you?" Dad asked.

"No," Zoe replied, in a quiet voice.

Dad narrowed his eyes. Zoe took a tiny sip of her gravy milk and said, "Yum."

When Dad left, Zoe growled, "You owe me a favour after covering for you!"

Chapter 4

Sliding into Trouble

Zoe shut herself alone in her bedroom. She was annoyed at Abby's prank, but she was also impressed – it was a pretty good one.

So, Zoe's next prank had to be bigger and better. Maybe even worthy of being on *Pranking Superstars*.

She finished the water in her bottle, trying to get the gravy flavour out of her mouth. Then she looked at the bottle in her hand and had another idea. It was Zoe's best idea yet!

Zoe went into the bathroom and filled up a spray bottle with water and soap. Then she sprayed the soapy water all over the tiles in the hallway.

Zoe stood in front of Abby's bedroom door and called out, "Abby! There's a cute dog walking past our house!"

Abby rushed out of her room, just like Zoe knew she would.

As soon as she did, Abby's bare feet skidded on the tiles.

But it wasn't funny.

Abby was out of control! She yelled "Help!", and her arms flew around like windmills.

Zoe watched, horrified, as her sister slid along the floor.

Abby kept slipping until she suddenly bumped into the hallway table and held on fast. The table wobbled, and the brown bag on it – the one with Grandma's gift inside – fell over.

The bag toppled onto the tiles. There was the sound of shattered glass. Then everything went quiet.

Abby and Zoe looked at each other in horror.

"Grandma's vase!" they yelled.

Mum and Dad rushed in. Dad stared down at the bag. "Were you two playing pranks on each other?"

Abby and Zoe nodded, and they burst into tears.

Chapter 5

The Final Prank

Abby and Zoe felt terrible. They helped Mum and Dad clean up the mess.
They even cleaned their rooms without being asked.

When Grandma finally came over, Abby and Zoe were very quiet.

Everyone sat at the dining table. Grandma read the birthday cards the girls had made for her.

"These are beautiful," Grandma said.

"Grandma, we broke the present we bought you," Abby said in a small voice. "I'm so sorry. We were being silly and playing pranks on each other." She started to cry.

"Goodness," Grandma said.

Mum and Dad looked at each other and grinned.

To the girls' surprise, Dad brought out another present from underneath the table. Grandma unwrapped it.

It was Abby and Zoe's vase!

"It's perfect!" Grandma said, with a big smile.

"But we broke it!" Zoe said, shocked.

"You broke some empty glass bottles," Dad replied.

"We took the bag with Grandma's vase from the hallway table earlier this morning to wrap it, and swapped it for a bag of recycling," Mum added. "We couldn't leave the vase out when you two were making so much trouble!"

"You *knew* we were pranking?" Abby said, surprised.

"And *you* pranked *us*?" Zoe was astonished.

Mum and Dad looked very proud.

"Well," Grandma said, laughing, "with all this talk about pranks, why don't you show me that *Pranking Superstars* you keep telling me about?"

Abby and Zoe looked at each other.

"I don't think we're in the mood for pranks anymore," Abby said.

"Totally," Zoe said. "Time to be a different kind of superstar!"